WICCA

GUIDED JOURNAL

*A Witch's Toolkit for Spiritual Discovery,
Sabbat Reflections, Spell Creations,
and Building Magical Skills*

LISA CHAMBERLAIN

Disclaimer

Your Free Gift

Thank you for adding this book to your Wiccan library! To learn more, why not join Lisa's Wiccan community and get an exclusive, free spell book?

The book is a great starting point for anyone looking to try their hand at practicing magic. The ten beginner-friendly spells can help you to create a positive atmosphere within your home, protect yourself from negativity, and attract love, health, and prosperity.

Little Book of Spells is now available to read on your laptop, phone, tablet, Kindle or Nook device!

To download, simply visit the following link:

www.wiccaliving.com/bonus

Also By Lisa Chamberlain

Wicca for Beginners: A Guide to Wiccan Beliefs, Rituals, Magic, and Witchcraft

Wicca Book of Spells: A Beginner's Book of Shadows for Wiccans, Witches, and Other Practitioners of Magic

Tarot for Beginners: A Guide to Psychic Tarot Reading, Real Tarot Card Meanings, and Simple Tarot Spreads

Runes for Beginners: A Guide to Reading Runes in Divination, Rune Magic, and the Meaning of the Elder Futhark Runes

Wicca Starter Kit: Wicca for Beginners, Finding Your Path, and Living a Magical Life

Wicca Spellbook Starter Kit: A Book of Candle, Crystal, and Herbal Spells

Wicca Herbal Magic: A Beginner's Guide to Herbal Spellcraft

Wicca Candle Magic: A Beginner's Guide to Candle Spellcraft

Wicca Crystal Magic: A Beginner's Guide to Crystal Spellcraft

Wiccan Kitchen: A Guide to Magical Cooking and Recipes

Wicca Moon Magic: A Wiccan's Guide and Grimoire for Working Magic with Lunar Energies

Wicca Wheel of the Year Magic: A Beginner's Guide to the Sabbats, with History, Symbolism, Celebration Ideas, and Dedicated Sabbat Spells

Wicca Book of Herbal Spells: A Book of Shadows for Wiccans, Witches, and Other Practitioners of Herbal Magic

Wicca Book of Candle Spells: A Book of Shadows for Wiccans, Witches, and Other Practitioners of Candle Magic

Wicca Book of Crystal Spells: A Book of Shadows for Wiccans, Witches, and Other Practitioners of Crystal Magic

Wicca Essential Oils Magic: A Beginner's Guide to Working with Magical Oils, with Simple Recipes and Spells

Wicca Elemental Magic: A Guide to the Elements, Witchcraft, and Magical Spells

3

*Wicca Magical Deities: A Guide to the Wiccan God and Goddess,
and Choosing a Deity to Work Magic With*

*Wicca Living a Magical Life: A Guide to Initiation
and Navigating Your Journey in the Craft*

*Magic and the Law of Attraction: A Witch's Guide to the Magic of Intention,
Raising Your Frequency, and Building Your Reality*

*Modern Witchcraft and Magic for Beginners: A Guide to Traditional and
Contemporary Paths, with Magical Techniques for the Beginner Witch*

Table of Contents

Introduction 6

How to use this book 7

Yule (Winter Solstice) 8

Synchronicity 16

Imbolc 24

New Moon 32

Ostara (Spring Equinox) 40

The Garden Path 48

Beltane 56

Animal Magic 64

Litha (Summer Solstice) 72

Bug Magic 80

Lammas 88

Focus Only On Your Desire 96

Mabon (Autumn Equinox) 104

Letting Go of "How" 112

Samhain 120

Full Moon 128

Turning the Wheel of the Year 136

Introduction

Welcome to the Wicca Guided Journal!

Here is your sanctuary for diving deep into your spiritual journey—the experiences, thoughts, and feelings that make up your unique, magical self. With a blend of blank writing pages and carefully crafted prompts to get you inspired, this journal is designed to help you discover and explore the authentic Witch within.

The writing prompts cover many aspects of the Wiccan experience, and are aimed at fostering your unique practice. For example: you've likely read several Wiccan authors' descriptions of the Goddess and the God, but how do **you** envision and experience these deities in your own life? What is your personal understanding of divine feminine and masculine energies? How would you describe your relationship with the Elements, or with Nature as a whole?

If you haven't given these things much thought before, you're not alone! But anyone who works with the Craft, Wiccan or otherwise, can benefit from exploring their inner relationship with the beliefs and practices of their chosen path. In this journal, you will find opportunities to examine your approach to magic, learn from what has worked well and what hasn't, forge stronger connections with your ritual and magical tools, work with the energies of Sabbats and lunar cycles, get clear on your magical intentions, and raise your vibrational frequency for more successful magic and more enjoyment of life.

How to use this book

This journal is designed to be flexible, so you can approach it in whatever way inspires you the most. The Sabbat prompts follow the order of the Wheel of the Year, so if you want to make it an annual book, you can save it for Yule (or Samhain, if that's the New Year for you) and start then. Or, you can start with whichever Sabbat is closest to you on the calendar right now. But there's no need to work with all of the prompts in linear order, unless you want to! Feel free to skip ahead to whatever inspires you in the moment, and come back around to earlier prompts later on. Or, take a divinatory approach: flip through the book at random, asking the Universe for guidance, and then write on the nearest prompt you land on. Again, this journal is your unique experience, so go with what speaks to *you*.

There are also plenty of blank, lined pages for you to use in any way you wish. You can create and record spells, write about your desires and magical goals, or even draw or paste in images and symbols that resonate with you in some way. (There are also several unlined blank pages at the end of the book for drawing!) One of my favorite things to write in my journals is what I call a "gratitude list." I simply list anything and everything I've appreciated about the past day, week, or month, from the smallest blessings to the big manifestations. An attitude of gratitude opens us up to further manifestations to come into our lives, so I recommend taking time regularly to intentionally reflect on what you've appreciated in the small moments of your days, as well as what is going well in your life in general. (You will find more detailed suggestions for this practice in the Lammas prompt of the journal.)

Keep in mind, also, that not everything you write about in the blank pages *has* to be directly related to an aspect of the Craft. If there are life issues you're struggling with, or situations you're seeking clarity on, you may find it helpful to write out your thoughts here. After all, our magic and our spiritual development are not separate from the rest of our daily lives, but directly influenced by them. So let your heart lead you through these pages, and enjoy the experience of reflection and discovery. May this journal guide your next steps along your magical path!

Blessed Be.

Yule (Winter Solstice)

Sabbat themes: *rebirth, quiet introspection, new year, hope, setting intentions, celebration of light.*

In many Wiccan traditions, Yule is the start of the new year. Many people see these short days and long nights as a time of self-reflection, spiritual study, and intention-setting for the coming year. This is a time of turning inward, hunkering down, and tuning in to our deepest selves.

What were some of your best moments or occasions of the past year? What lessons, if any, have you learned about yourself, or about life in general, since last Yule? How has your spiritual practice developed? What would you like to see in your life in the year to come? What are your hopes for the world, going forward?

What is your experience of meditation like? Do you get frustrated with your wandering mind? Do you receive insights "out of the blue"? (A little bit of both?) How do you feel after meditating? What do you notice about how it impacts the rest of your day (or your sleep, if you meditate at night)? If you don't meditate regularly, set a goal of doing so for 10–15 minutes per day for the next five days. Then write about your experiences here.

Synchronicity

Psychologist and mystic Carl Jung coined the term "synchronicity" to describe meaningful and mysterious coincidences in our lives that seem to be trying to tell us something. Some examples are seeing repeating number patterns or repeating symbols, or more significant events like running into someone you were just thinking about. Synchronicities are one way that the Law of Attraction manifests in our lives.

Think of some memorable synchronicities you've experienced. Why were they significant? Do these events have anything in common? What do you think the Universe may have been trying to tell you?

Do you have a favorite Sabbat? Which is it, and why is it your favorite? If you don't have a clear favorite Sabbat, which ones do you especially enjoy celebrating, and why?

Imbolc

Purification is a central focus at Imbolc, stemming from the old days when dwellings had to be shut tight against the cold for months. At the first sign of thaw, it was time to throw open the doors and cleanse the house of the stuffy, stale air. Sunlight was also a purifying force—a manifestation of the Element of Fire—and was taken advantage of as much as possible for renewing the body and the spirit.

What aspects of your life could use a good clearing out at this time? Is there a closet full of stuff you never use that could be put to better use by someone else? Are there toxic friendships that you would benefit from letting go of? Could you use a good physical cleanse or detox process? Identify the areas of your life that feel bogged down by old energy. What can you do to release the old and make room for new blessings to come in with the beginnings of Spring?

How do you envision or perceive the Goddess? What is your personal understanding of divine feminine energy? When you think of the Goddess, is she a human-looking being that can be visually percieved, or is your conception something more nebulous? How do you tap into or commune with her energy?

New Moon

The New Moon is an ideal time for dreaming of what you wish to create in your life. What do you want to manifest over the coming weeks and months? What kind(s) of spellwork might you employ? What are some action steps you can take on the material plane to help things along?

(Note: feel free to repeat this writing process at each New Moon. You can designate any of the blank pages in the journal for New Moon writing.)

Which aspect(s) of the Goddess do you incorporate into your practice? Why do you resonate with these particular goddesses? Which ancient culture(s) do they come from? Is there a particular myth they appear in that speaks to you on a personal level? If you don't work with individual aspects, why not?

_____

_____

_____

_____

_____

_____

_____

_____

_____

_____

_____

_____

_____

_____

_____

_____

_____

_____

_____

Ostara (Spring Equinox)

Sabbat themes: *balance, renewal, action, beginnings, hope, new possibilities.*

At Ostara, the fertility of the Earth becomes more and more undeniable as the slow energies of winter give way to the fresh new vibrancy of spring. As the first green shoots poke up through the soil, we truly begin the active half of the Wheel of the Year, turning our focus to outward action, new life, and fresh starts.

What seeds would you like to plant in your life at this time? What areas of your practice would you like to develop further? Identify 3 goals you'd like to work for over the coming growing season, and brainstorm ways that you can get started. What action(s) can you take today to get things moving in a new direction? What can you do within the next week? What can you do over the coming month?

What has been your most successful spell so far? What was the goal you worked for and what were the results? Why do you think it was successful? What can you apply from this experience to future spellwork?

The Garden Path

Not all Witches are "Green Witches" with glorious gardens, but most of us have at least a houseplant or two, or some modest potted herbs. Write about your experiences with growing plants. What have been your successes in this area? What obstacles have you encountered? If you had the ideal amount of space and sunlight, what would you grow, and why? What's a step you can take now toward bringing more plant energy into your daily life?

What has been your least successful spell so far? What might be some reasons for why it didn't/hasn't worked? One common reason is that we aren't actually clear on our intentions when working the spell. Use this opportunity to reflect on what it is you truly wanted to get out of the spell. Is your desire still the same now, or has something changed?

Beltane

Sabbat themes: *passion, mischief, sensuality, sexuality, beauty, romance, fertility, vitality, abundance.*

Wiccans recognize Beltane as a time to celebrate the return of passion, vitality, fun and frivolity, and the co-creative energies of Nature that are so evident at this time of year. By this point all living creatures have come out of hibernation and are enjoying the sunshine and the mild days.

Humans differ from the rest of Nature in that we are the only species to tailor our behavior based on the opinions of others (or our perception of the opinions of others). Animals live a completely free existence in this respect—they are always entirely themselves. Where do you hold yourself back due to social expectations or peer pressure (real or perceived)? If you could be your most true, authentic self in front of the whole world, with absolutely no consequences (other than feeling completely free and alive), what would that look like for you?

How do you envision or perceive the God? What is your personal understanding of divine masculine energy? When you think of the God, is he a human-looking being that can be visually percieved, or is your conception something more nebulous? How do you tap into or commune with his energy?

Animal Magic

Many Witches work with animals, whether in the form of "familiars," "animal spirit guides," or some other spiritual concept. You may already have spiritual connections with one or more animals, or you may not have explored this area of practice before. Either way, take this opportunity to get more up-close with animal energy by writing about one.

What's your favorite non-domesticated animal? (If you don't have one, try adopting one temporarily for the purposes of this journal entry.) Do a bit of research on this animal from scientific sources and record at least 7 facts about it that you find interesting or significant. Why does this animal appeal to you personally?

Then, consult some spiritual sources on animal guides and read about this animal's symbolism, magical associations, energetic qualities, etc. How do these associations connect with you personally? What kind of connection do you feel to this animal now (if any)?

If you like to draw, consider including a sketch or drawing of this animal. Or, you can print out an image you like and paste it somewhere on the page.

Which aspect(s) of the God do you incorporate into your practice? Why do you resonate with these particular gods? Which ancient culture(s) do they come from? Is there a particular myth they appear in that speaks to you on a personal level? If you don't work with individual aspects, why not?

Litha (Summer Solstice)

Sabbat themes: *abundance, growth, masculine energy, love, magic.*

Litha is the height of summer, when the days are warm and plentiful. Abundance can be found everywhere, as the crops are in full growth and the fields and forests are bursting with animal and plant life. This is the time of the God's greatest power, whether we focus on the light and heat of his Sun God aspect; his role as the Green Man, lush with thick foliage; or the Horned God, strong and agile at the heart of the forest. At the same time, the Goddess is in her Mother aspect, as the generous Earth yields abundant blessings of food, flowers, and striking natural beauty.

In our modern culture, we tend to think of abundance in terms of money and financial security. But money is largely just a means to the things we want an abundance of, like food, clothing, and access to enjoyable activities. There are also many forms of non-material abundance, such as good health, friendships, love, restful sleep, free time, etc. Where in your life are you already abundant? Where would you like to create more abundance in the near future?

What does your wand do for you? How do you utilize it in ritual and/or magic? How do you feel when using it? (If you don't use a wand in your practice, what do you use instead, and why?)

Bug Magic

When it comes to the topic of animal guides or animal magic, the smallest creatures of all often get overshadowed. Spiders certainly have their place in the hearts of many Witches, and everyone loves fireflies, but on the whole, insects and arachnids tend not to come to mind when we're thinking about the spiritual aspects of animals. Yet there's plenty to learn from the energies of these tiny beings.

You may or may not have a favorite insect (or arachnid), but if you don't, try adopting one temporarily for the purposes of this journal entry. Do a bit of research on this animal from scientific sources and record at least 3 facts about it that you find interesting or significant. Why does this insect interest you personally?

Then, consult some spiritual sources on animal guides and read about this insect's symbolism, magical associations, energetic qualities, etc. How do these associations connect with you personally? What kind of connection do you feel to this insect now (if any)?

If you like to draw, include a sketch or drawing of this insect. Or, you can print out an image you like and paste it somewhere on the page.

What does "sacred space" mean for you? How do you create it in your practice? What do you notice about the energy of the circle (if you cast circles) or other sacred space that's different from your normal, everyday experience?

_____

_____

_____

_____

_____

_____

_____

_____

_____

_____

_____

_____

_____

_____

_____

_____

_____

_____

Lammas

Sabbat themes: *first fruits, harvest, gratitude, benevolent sacrifice, utilizing skills and talents.*

Lammas is the time of the "first fruits" and is known in Wiccan and other Pagan traditions as the first of the three harvest festivals. This is a time to consciously recognize the fruits of our labors—whether literally or metaphorically—and to give thanks for all that has manifested.

Appreciating what is going well in your life is key to manifesting more of it. Gratitude lists are a popular practice for many spiritual seekers, including many Witches who include them as part of their Full Moon celebrations. But gratitude doesn't have to be just about the "big" things, like financial security or love. In fact, appreciating the "little" things in each day—like smooth traffic on the way to work, or a break in the rain just when you need to run outside for a moment—is what truly helps us raise our vibrational frequency, which in turn allows for more of those big things to manifest in our lives!

What do you appreciate about your life at the moment? See how many aspects of your experience you can think of that have brought you satisfaction or joy. Be sure to include things you have accomplished through your own efforts. (Again, these can also be large or small. We often don't give ourselves enough credit for simply doing the dishes or eating a healthy meal.) Give yourself appreciation here for anything you do in the process of co-creating your magical life. And take note of how you feel at the end of this writing. How has your mood shifted? Did new items come to mind more easily as you got some momentum going?

Describe one of your favorite places in Nature. This can be somewhere close to home, somewhere you visit a lot, or somewhere you've only been to once. Be as descriptive as you can, painting a picture of this place with your words. How did/do you feel in this place? How did/does being there connect you to your spiritual practice?

Focus Only On Your Desire

One obstacle to successful spellwork is an inability to truly focus on what you want without also thinking about the fact that you *don't* have it right *now*. (For example, if you're working a spell for a new job, but are feeling anxious about how much you need a job while you're working the spell, it's unlikely to produce results.)

You can help yourself avoid this counteractive energy by doing some freewriting before the spellwork begins. Acknowledge your concerns about the issue, and then declare your intention to leave them out of the picture for the time being. Then, shift your focus to what you truly want, and not merely what seems possible for you at the moment. Focus only on the details about it that you desire, and write about it as if it has already come to be. For example, in the above scenario, you might write "I love how this job challenges me in new ways," or "the people I work with are fun to be around." Take note of how this exercise shifts your mood and, more importantly, your vibrational frequency. Do you feel more prepared now to cast a successful spell?

What's a natural environment you've never seen in person but would like to (such as the mountains, the desert, or the ocean)? Write about this kind of environment. What intrigues you about the natural phenomenon in this place? How do you imagine you would feel there?

Mabon (Autumn Equinox)

Sabbat themes: *harvest, gratitude, abundance, balance, preparation, welcoming the dark.*

For many people, Mabon is a bittersweet moment, as the shortening days and color-changing leaves remind us that we're heading into colder and darker times. But this is the true essence of the seasons and the Wheel— all of creation is always in motion, and the only constant in life is change.

What changes do you notice in the outer environment at this time of the Autumn Equinox? What changes do you notice in yourself, and/or in your spiritual practice? What do you appreciate about the darker, colder months of the year? What would you like to focus on in your practice over the coming months?

Is there an Element you resonate with more than all the others? Why is it your favorite Element? Write about your experiences communing with the energy of this Element, and/or working with this Element in magic. (If you don't have a clear favorite Element, choose one that particularly interests you at the moment to write about.)

Letting Go of "How"

Another habit of thought that gets in the way of successful manifestation is trying to figure out *how* what you want is going to happen. For example, when it comes to attaining wealth, many people think they need to either win the lottery, marry into wealth, or inherit a fortune through some mysterious relative. This belief causes them to block out the literally infinite number of other ways that money could come into their lives. The trick is to leave the "how" out of the equation, and let the Universe sort it out.

One way to do this is to shift your focus to answering *why* you want what you want. What will you gain from manifesting this particular desire? What in your life do you think will change? How will you feel? Spend some time freewriting about this, creating a vision for your life that brings you joy, and leave the "how" to the Universe. Then, if you feel so inspired, try a spell related to your goal.

Many of us have kept an interesting rock or a pretty shell that we've kept with us from some special place or occasion in our lives. Describe a natural object that's significant to you, in as much detail as you can. What is the story surrounding it? How do you feel when you hold or look at it? Why do you think you've kept it for as long as you have?

Samhain

Sabbat themes: *death, rebirth, divination, honoring ancestors, introspection, benign mischief, revelry.*

Samhain is often described as the night when "the veil between the worlds is at its thinnest," and many choose to honor their ancestors and other departed loved ones at this time.

How much do you know about your own ancestors? Who were the oldest living relatives you knew as a child, and what, if anything, did you learn from them? Have you inherited any gifts or talents from your family lineage? Are there any ancestral patterns you would like to transform or heal during your lifetime?

Alternatively, you can write a letter to the ancestors you never knew in your lifetime. Ask them any questions you'd like to know the answers to. What would you like them to know about you?

Describe a time when you felt very connected with the spirit world. What did you notice or think about during that moment? What was different about it from your ordinary experience?

Full Moon

The Full Moon is the most powerful phase of the entire lunar cycle. Magic related to particularly important goals is often worked at this time. As you prepare to celebrate the Full Moon, you may wish to write a list of all that has benefited you over the past month and express your appreciation for these blessings. Doing so before making any new magical requests is a great way to honor the Full Moon theme of abundance. It also helps you raise your vibrational frequency to an optimal state before sending out your new intention.

(Note: feel free to repeat this writing process at each Full Moon. You can designate any of the blank pages in the journal for Full Moon writing.)

Write about a spell ingredient you use a lot. What do you like about incorporating it into your magic? What is its particular resonance or significance for you? What spells have you used it in and what have been the results so far?

_____

_____

_____

_____

_____

_____

_____

_____

_____

_____

_____

_____

_____

_____

_____

_____

_____

_____

_____

Turning the Wheel of the Year

Looking back on the last year, what have been your major lessons, or areas of development, along your spiritual path? What major events, whether personal or collective, have motivated you to increase your magical and/or intuitive skills? Going forward, what areas of the Craft do you want to explore further? If you wish, write about your goals for the next cycle of the Wheel of the Year.

Printed in the USA
CPSIA information can be obtained
at www.ICGtesting.com
LVHW022246291023
762509LV00003B/11

9 781912 715800